My Soul
is a Broken Down Valise

Rob Plath

First edition. Printed in the USA.

ISBN: 978-1-926860-68-8

Some of these poems originally appeared in Tapping Ashes In The Dark (Lummox Press) and Staring Down Your Wounds (Epic Rites Press).

Epic Rites Press publications are distributed worldwide by Tree Killer Ink. For more information about *My Soul Is A Broken Down Valise* (and other books and publications from Epic Rites Press) please visit the Epic Rites website at www.epicrites.org.

Epic Rites: any press is only as "small" as its thinking

Contents

My Soul
is a Broken Down Valise

Rob Plath

This book is dedicated to Wolfgang
Motherfucking Carstens & Death...

poet laureate of landfills

i am poet laureate
of the landfills
of tons of dead tvs
billions of coffee grinds
& blobs of worn prophylactics
of seagulls & fat rats
i sift thru
empty beer bottles
& tuna cans for my verse
ragged tin tops
slice my hands
i bleed on eternal styrofoam
of crushed egg cartons
i sleep on torn mattresses
w/ coils that bite
my calves like snakes
at dawn i sing of
noise polluted hydraulics
of garbage trucks

the price

b/c
the wheel
spins
too much
inside
the electric
meter box
on the
outside of
the house
a father beats
his son
w/ in
its walls
where bones
are broken
more than
bread
sounds
fucked up
but it's
the price
we pay
for the
birth of
a true
fucking
poet

a good raw poem

a good raw poem
is much needed
at times
of literary freeze
it's a zippo lighter
flame on high
beneath the frozen
sack of black juice
in yr torso
it's a keg tap
on yr spleen
don't ever fucking knock
the good raw poem
one day when
yr literary
vision
is full
of cataracts
you'll scream for
the edge of
a good raw poem
to slide across
yr corneas
let some goddamn
light in

mascot of poetry

i woke myself
coughing
i had half
a glass of water
next to my bed
i spit what was
in my mouth
into it
the glob floated
half below
& half on
the surface
like a small
yellowish
jellyfish
w/ one eye
of blood
at the center
the mascot
of my poetry

unwanted ink

you keep writing
yr award-winning poems
you keep writing
yr grant fuelled poems
yr shiny trophy poems
you keep in a glass case
beneath the wall of diplomas
& i'll keep writing
my atrophied poems
my blacklisted poems
america's most unwanted poems
poems that those in power
want to erase like unwelcomed ink
etched into the flesh

my spit cup

i am sick
i keep a cup
near the bed to
spit in
a spit cup
b/c i'm too
lazy to get up
& hack in the
toilet bowl
as the night
goes on
the cup gets
higher
this is the only
case in which
my own glass
is "half full"
as the optimist's
platitude preaches
the cup is filling
w/ poems
in the night
sometimes ten poems
by morning
most poets say
that poetry is
a love of words
i beg to
fucking differ
poetry is born
long before it hits
the white page
it is born deep

in the branches of
the wheezing lung-sacks
in the gut, the bowels
& these organs are
not pretty pink things
they are odious
they are slimy
they are oozing
have you ever had
the pleasure of taking
a whiff of an open
body cavity
i have
until you do keep
playing w/ yr words
& yrself

feeling lucky

it's late march
10:08 pm

i have my car window
lowered for the first
time in a while

my right palm rests
across the bottom
of the wheel

the other holds
a fresh cigarette

sitting at a red light
tapping the ashes
out into the dark
i think for a moment
of all the men
spending their first night
in their graves

& then all four
strings of traffic lights
flash green

so i punch the gas
& the guts
of my old car
pull me thru

unloading poems

don't be a dictator
you gotta unload them whatever way they
demand
this one might be a grocery list
this one a sermon of bile
this one just a straight story
(& don't be a fool, those count too)
you gotta ejaculate them whatever way they
demand
this one might be a post-it note
this one a bureaucratic form
this one a mad repeater, a crazy blood machine
you gotta launch them whichever way they
they demand
this one might be schizophrenic, a pimped out
childhood memory
or a truck driver mouthed prayer
this one just plain ingredients
this one a fucked up joke that
leaves you w/ enemies
a warning sticker
a death notice
a money shot
a beer shit
an autopsy

barbed poetry

one night i was drunk & ate pumpkin seeds
i had that ferocious wine hunger
i didn't shell them
in fact, i hardly chewed them
my fingers were coordinating enough to
just move from bag to mouth
the next day i suffered tho
first came the shells like tiny thorns
passing thru the asshole
a wincing barbed wire shit
then the paper w/ streaks of shit & blood
that's a fucking metaphor for poetry
if there ever was one
devouring the world in big gulps
w/out preparing it first
w/out safely stripping it to the soft seed
then letting the barbs rip thru you
squeezing out blood & shit on the page

a new poetry machine

i got a new typing machine
a new poetry machine
& got rid of the old one
after six years
i donated the old one
to a thrift shop
except the keyboard
call me superstitious
or demented
but i heard a voice like
bukowski's saying:
if you smash it, a shitload
of more poems will come
so i smashed it
w/ a hammer
the keys popped
off at me
the loud whapping of
the head of the hammer
was like gunfire
i swear the first key
that flew off was F
i smashed it again & again
until most of the keys
ricocheted off the walls
then i took it & broke it
in half over my knee
bent it right in fucking half
like closing an old book shut
in order to open a new one

poetry: a definition

i've always
felt the function
of poetry
was to delay
suicide
that poems
had to be
simple straight
talk
for instance,
like what'd
you'd say
to someone
from an
open window
while they
are on
the ledge
ten stories
up from pavement
anything else,
according to
this definition,
is equivalent
to pushing
the fucker

my poetry

i am
owner
of a
brutal lantern
it glides
over
the dark
waters
in my skull
the crabs
of pain
surface
in its
flush
& soon
after
their shells
whistle
in the
boiling pot

the blade

my father prided himself on being
a thug, a leg breaker, a thief
whose every third word was cunt or
motherfucker
& usually aimed at his own family
but he wouldn't allow his twelve year-old son
to have a miniature swiss army knife
i remember he grabbed it from my hands
& kept it himself in the drawer
w/ other larger knives & a pistol
i loved the knife back then
the way it snapped in & out of its
thin bed
but when i grew older & disinterested
in knives & bb guns, etc
i found i possessed another kind of edge
passed down to me thru the centuries
a beautiful blade sheathed in the skull
which grows sharper & sharper
& never is in need of the grindstone

belts of nails

lay down the line
sharper, harder, pal
lay down something
that resembles those
spike-strips that the police
lay out on the road
to bring a high speed chase
to its end
steal their tools
but steer clear
of the cop-soul
be the outlaw in the car
they're chasing
lay down the line, pal
belts of nails

meditation on smoking

i like the way the lighter kick starts beneath my
thumb & cuts the darkness
i like the way the cherry ember glows beneath
my nose leading the path to nowhere
i like the way smoke gets pulled into the wind as
i stand on the old patio
i like the way smoke hits the large bookshelf then
spreads out like the tree of no-knowledge
i like the way the smoke curls up thru the lamp
shades like genie-hobos w/ empty pockets
i like the way i can stick my fist thru the thick
cloud in the tiny living room
i like the way the sulfur smells like the devil
when i wave the wooden match out
i like the way the smoke goes out the window
like an escaped convict
i like the way the cigars wait in their box like
unborn children
i like the way smoke repels a fly when i blow it at
its dark wings
i like the way smoke sits in the sunrays like a
decrepit gray rainbow
i like the way smoke hangs like a map of the
place i came from before i was born
i like the way the cigar cannibalizes itself as it sits
in the groove of the ashtray
i like the way smoke hangs in the air justifying
my laziness
i like the way smoke sits & waits, sad ether, if the
windows are shut
i like the way the red hot tip shows how flimsy
flesh is when i hold the cherry against my palm

i like the way the ashes fold at the tip like a tiny
animal brain
i like the way the stubs accumulate in the ashtray
like tiny buckled water pipes
i like the way the way the outer leaf unravels like
a miniature nervous breakdown
i like the way smoke flows upward like a crazy
maverick stream
i like the way smoke slips into the braids of the
rug
i like the way smoke haunts the fibers of my shirt
i like the way smoke clouds my face in the mirror
while washing my hands
i like the way smoke sits in the center of the room
like a fat gray buddha
i like the way the smoke smell comes out of my
copy of schopenhauer
i like the way smoke uncurls from my mouth like
the great silent tongue of god

the temper

once when i was eight
my father was driving us
to long beach to visit
some aunts & uncles

it was a hot june morning
when we got to the town.
my father stopped at a bakery
to get a box of pastries

as we pulled away from the curb
a man cut us off

my father zoomed thru cars
to catch up to him
he pulled right next to the man
at a red light
& asked my mother to roll
the window all the way down
then he screamed over her,
"i've got kids in the backseat,
you stupid fuck. i'll get out
& break yr fucking head
open, you motherfucker!"
the guy kept his head straight
& didn't look over

we were all silent

the light changed & my father
punched the gas pedal
& the car
jumped forward

black wires & cigarette burns

she used to say that
my birthmarks
(i have many)
were constellations
& she'd press her
finger to each one
& try to connect them
she'd grab the dark hairs
that covered my forearms
twist & play w/ them
run them between her fingers
call me her wolf
but now my birthmarks are
all cigarette burns again
& my forearms are covered
w/ black wires again

the young poet

every
morning
he hacked
up
what was
sitting
at the
back
of his
throat
& spit
it onto the
telephone
pole
at the
bus stop
dozens of
different
shaped
petrified
white
phlegm
balls
most
of them
w/ an eye
of blood
at the
center
frozen
to the
wooden
post

as the ugly
yellow
bus
came
to eat
us up

pulling down wallpaper

pulling down
wallpaper
in the kitchen
i haven't had a drink
in a week
a cigar
in two weeks
thought it'd be easy
but the old paper
splits in half
leaves behind a layer
here & there
or if it does come off
in one piece
there's a splotch
of the paste
frozen to the wall
peeling off the second layer
reminds me of
peeling skin off
my sunburned shoulders
as a kid
those tissue-like
shreds that
i'd roll into a ball
& flick on the floor
there are lots of
hidden screw holes
beneath the paper
tiny black punctures
that once held something
sometimes i peel
a slice of paper off

& it takes a layer or two
of paint w/ it
revealing a sickly green
beneath the two white coats
in other places
the spackling tape
runs visible
or the arcs of the hammer
& bent heads of nails

light & bread

one of my struts is loose
i have a filthy air filter
& a slow leak in
the right front tire
i feel alone like a sparrow
in a cat's mouth
no-one notices
that cat & its fangs sunk
in me as i stand in line
at the supermarket
w/ a box of light bulbs
& a loaf of bread
light & bread
in the cat's mouth
my twenty year-old car
rides rough like the lugs
are screwed to four skulls
there's a kfc
being built on the corner
across from terry brother's tire
rubber & chicken boiling in oil
i park across the street
from my apartment
b/c the landlady doesn't
want me blocking her flowers
inside i proceed to light a cigar
twist bulbs into empty sockets
of two lamps
butter three slices of bread
& roll down the blinds
as the cat's grip loosens a little

the broken record

in this life
we're wired
between two fat zeros

the first O
is our mama's twat
& the second, of course
is the death-hole

twat...rot...twat...rot...twat...rot

the real fucking music
of the spheres

card tables & makeshift ashtrays

i am hysterical
altho i appear
still & soundless
quietly smoking cigarettes
but you can be hysterical
w/out screaming
you can be hysterical
just say
gathering smoke
into yr lungs
or flicking an ash
in a small room
in broad daylight
my mind is rickety
like a card table
it can hold maybe
a makeshift tincan ashtray
a pack of cigarettes
a blue bic lighter
my elbow
& as i sit here
the table is mostly bare
mostly empty space
a little shaky
one day death will put its fist
right thru this table
as easy as plunging
it thru the smoke
that floats above it
& it'll put its fist right thru
yr colossal table too
right thru the fancy centerpiece
the big fat candleholders

thick plates & colorful glasses
the solid napkin rings
the shiny, heavy utensils
right on thru the ample
wooden top

batting stones

when i was thirteen
i had a friend phil who
was an altar boy
one time i remember
phil had stolen that metal plate
w/ the long handle
that he used to hold
beneath parishioners' chins
as the priest placed
the communion wafer
on their tongues
the shiny plate was there
just in case the eucharist fell
it would not hit the unclean floor
i remember we took the thing
into the woods one night
& crept up to backyard fences
of homes in our neighborhood
we used it to hit stones at houses
we swung that thing hard
like it was a baseball bat
i remember the clang of stone
on metal & then a few seconds
of silence, then the knock of the rock
on the roof, & then it tumbling down
sometimes hitting off the gutter
before it dropped
we kept moving along the edge
of the woods, batting stones
at the lit up houses
i remember it was starless
we were two angry kids
his father was dead

mine was living
but i wished he were dead
it felt good to swing that stupid
thing from the church
& hear the stones come down
on the rooftops
near the end of our night
we hit a window
& heard the glass shatter
a man came out in the dark
he was cursing
screaming into the darkness
that he was going to beat the shit
out of us
if he found us
we laughed & then made our way
thru the woods
phil leading the way
using the stolen weapon
like an ax, chopping
at the branches as we walked
back to our own houses

the unstoppable belt of the grinder

i had to take the tank
off of the toilet
to put in new parts
but the bolts were
rusted after many years
& i couldn't get them off
so i broke out the grinder
& ground them off
sparks flew everywhere
bits of bolts
i finally got the tank off
& put the new parts in
& bolted it back
but as i was washing
rust & grease off
of my hands, i looked
at my unshaven face
in the mirror
the dark gouges
beneath my eyes,
new lines etched
around them,
more gray
in the sideburns
then i looked down
as i dried my hands
at the bits of bolts
on the ground,
the shavings,
the steel dust

a new kind of movement

i'm not sure
if i move anymore

in the literal
sense of the word
that is…

it seems the more exact
verb would be spill

i spill out of bed
i spill across the room
i spill into the street

not like hot fresh blood
or electric pearly seed

or any kind of water
or holy oil

i can't compare it
to any particular form

it's just like a pure surrender
if such a thing

no wishes

you stare down at
four burned out
romeo y julieta
cigar stubs
five silver beer
bottle caps

shining thru
a mound of ash
in the ashtray

you grab the
longest stub

the one you were
smoking last

before you got up
to take a piss

& revive it
between yr lips

w/ the last match

you draw in
long & good

then blow out hard

sighing simultaneously

watching the smoke
spreading across

the small room

swirling up thru
the green lampshade

rising out of the top
like a genie
w/out any wishes
to grant you

1969

in 1969 i slowly grew
w/ in a blood cocoon
in my mother's womb

in that unsound-proof room
the noose of the umbilical
fed me first-hand clouds
of chain-smoked cigarettes

while the outer world
of tough brooklyn
sent me a daily barrage
of my father's curse words

cunt, motherfucker, bastard, whore
sandwiched between puffs of no-filters
a broken record of smoking & swearing

this is how i grew
while somewhere out there
the poor flower children began to wilt

absurd peepholes

two eyes

in between
two sides
of the abyss

looking back
& weeping

gazing ahead
& trembling

two eyes

sandwiched
between
two slices
of darkness

shut them
tight tonight

close the absurd
peepholes

bursting

there
is
an
invalid
slowly
waking
up
in
you

&
behind
that,
a cadaver

&
behind
that,
a
star...

chuckling clay

i'm sick of vacuuming
my own dead flesh

i'm sick of picking off
the remaining flakes
from my frame

i want a parade
not a funeral

i want to jump in
my stripped off skin
that lay too long
like a deflated balloon

zipper it up
over these moaning
bones

not a body bag
like in the past

but a laughing
suit of flesh

a coat of
chuckling clay

encompass

the cat sits
on the sill

all four paws
tucked under
her shape

looking like
a squat
furry boat

stationary
& pleased

envy

driving down
the road tonight
i saw the red
reflectors
flashing from
bicycle pedals
as i got closer
i saw the boy
riding the bike
then i made out
his friend
standing on
the back pegs
w/ his hands
on his friend's
shoulders
hair blowing in
the wind
oh, to be that
boy again
so young
flying down
the streetlampless
road
standing
not even
pedaling
cutting my shape
into
the wind

farther than all the bridges i've ever burned

i write like my life
there's not much in it

but what little there is, is larger
than all the pounds of fat i've cut away

farther reaching than all the bridges i've burned

higher than all the dreams i've crushed
beneath my own feet, etc...

one man standing
stripped down to the basic frame

his spleen dripping w/ bile in one hand
a paintbrush in the other...

for the flames

come to think of it now
i never loved any

their skins & commitments
were sacrificial

fuel for the flames
of my inner singular love

hemorrhaging in the modern age

i used to pour
so much whiskey
into myself

my innards
were coated
in thick amber

my pain perfectly
preserved for study

my prehistoric
guts

not meant
for this
age

i think it still has teeth

i've pistol whipped
the universe
for 40 years

until its cheek bones
cracked

its eyes closed up

& it lay slumped
in a chair

maybe it's time
i cut the duct tape
that secures its arms
keeps its spine
against the cold rungs

maybe it needs
to be set free
in my heart

perhaps it's time to break
out the emergency kit
& fix it up

i think it still has teeth
to smile w/ at me

a forgiving grin

i'll know when i've reached the line

just like i am finished w/ a book
finished w/ a smoke
finished w/ a love
what if i am finished w/ a life?

what do i do if it ends before it has
chronologically ended?

do i pull a van gogh, muzzle to gut?

so many people think they're unfinished
w/ life even on their deathbed

when in actuality, long before
its cover had closed
its cherry had traveled down to the filter
& love had skated down the toilet

in all my dying loves

the other night
while driving
my high beams hit
the still-open eyes
of roadkill
on the dark shoulder
& there shined a light
from w/ in the pile of rot
& i gunned it then
b/c it reminded me
of the false hope
gleaming in
all my dying loves

july beauties

the july beauties pose
on fine white sand

their meat covering
the bone much better
than most

these shining shapes
well-oiled, polished
w/ not one edge

i'm amazed by this
trick of the magic skin
diverting us from
the framework
the marrow

even their smiles
their teeth, so full
of seductive promises
you'd never believe
they're merely
chips of bone

just my guts as i whirl

wandering away
from waterfalls
of whiskey

& clouds of
cigarette smoke
etc…

no crutches

just my guts
holding me up

as i juggle both
darkness & light

both laughter
& dissolution

until they are but
one thing turning

like a great blinking
ferris wheel
above my head

as the planet
whirls 1,200 mph
on its axis

love, lust & lame drunk dogs

love sneaks in
to our bedroom
every night
& replaces the
solid knobs of
our spines
w/ discs of dust
that seem solid
at first
but they crumble
eventually
when we walk
about & attempt
to move the fuck
on
& there we lie
collapsed
on our own floor
lapping whiskey
like a lame dog

love poem

i chain-smoked
yr wrists
& didn't hack

i put yr
eyeballs out
on my palms
& didn't
blister

i swung
from a
noose
of yr
thick hair
& my neck
stayed intact

i wore
a bag of
yr skin
around my
whole head
& didn't
turn blue

i dropped
shots of
yr bile
into pint
glasses
of yr blood
& didn't get
the spins

maybe just maybe

saw a photo of me
at 6 years old
clutching a baseball bat

legs spread
ready to whack
the leather ball

happy just to be able
to exert my musculature
under then summer sun

my thin hairless arms flexed
eyes wide & waiting

my heart was an apple
for christsakes
not a fist dunked in blood

shit, no wet dreams
yet—girls were boys to me

i even thought they
had ding-a-lings too

tits & booze & smoke
were farther away
than the stars

bats were for balls not bones
& stitches to finger before a pitch

i believe i was happy
in that photograph

i braille the kodak paper
from 1974

the edges unbent
the colors still vibrant

maybe there's still hope
just maybe…

misfit living

there has always been
the minimal here

no dining room set
no living room set
no kitchen set
no children's beds
etc…

no purchases of newness
no uniformity

only rickety card-tables
third-hand chairs & shelves
hand-me-downs
from the dead

faded, mismatched
chipped & scratched

a roomful of misfit sticks
of furniture

& to top it off
an old mattress upon the floor
the lopsided raft
of a capsized soul
going nowhere

just floating…

no-one's immune from the detonation of a kiss

i see a young handsome man who seems
untouched by tragedy
hand-in-hand w/ his beautiful girl walking thru
the café doors
& kissing leaning upon the thick lip of the
wooden bar
he has his whiskey, his woman, these summers,
these nights
his hand moving over her hip — a sliver of flesh
heaven
but sitting in the shadows i see visions they
won't ever see until it's too late
his live hand grenade heart, her thin finger
locked inside the ring of the pin
i continue sitting & sketching the scene before
the eventual blast

peak experience

sitting in early morning
staring at the kitchen counter
everything silent
the microwave
the blender
the toaster
the coffee machine
the radio
all just resting there
like stage props
replicas
w/ out real workable
guts w/ in
even the refrigerator
is momentarily quiet
nothing is gurgling
or humming
or mincing
or popping
& even the cupboards sit or hang there
their doors & drawers appearing glued shut
their silver knobs seeming
ornamental rather than practical
like a pocket on a coat
that is merely for show
& the only thing that
is moving & causing any noise
is the clock's big hand
making its way around its face
a steady ticking
an endless passage
its innards alive
turning & turning & turning

precisely

the
old
hobo
grins

b/c
he
has
no
teeth

pick ax philosophy

if
you
dig
deep
enough

you'll
always
hit
agony

the
core
of
mankind

happiness
is
a
surface
thing

exists
only
w/in
the
first
few
layers

anything
beneath
is

mouthfuls
of
dust

then
all
fire

**something the killer human heart will never
learn**

the flower lovers are really stomping
upon the flowers they say they love
just as much as the haters of flowers
who crush them under the soles of their boots

the way they sort & categorize them
the way they dissect them, naming their parts
the way they pin labels upon them
the way they bow to them & praise them
the way they capture them & fence them in
the way they twist them into bouquets or
wreaths

flowers just want to stand & be
wild & nameless
something the killer heart will never learn

flowers do not mourn at funerals
or weep w/ joy at weddings

one day when the mushroom clouds of doom
bloom all around
the roses will just stand there

neither sad nor happy

songs nobody will hear

the corpses are full of music
songs nobody will hear

their music bounces off
the sides of coffins

sometimes slipping
past the nailed lids

but never past the 6 foot
sound-proof dirt rooms

these corpses full of music
emit the same song over & over

songs they never sang in life
songs only the worms hear

staring down yr wounds

i remember once
a few years before
her death
my grandmother
had an operation
& afterwards the doctor
wanted her to look
at where the long incision
was on her side
to confront the stitches
but my grandmother refused
she never looked
she said that knowing it
was there was enough
& i understand her fear
it's one thing to know it's
there
but to confront the zigzag
zipper of stitches sewn
into yr skin
to stare down yr wounds
to braille yr scars
is something else, yes, it is
something far different

sunday morning

my cat sprawled
across
the old wooden
windowsill

her fuzzy rib cage
rising
& falling

while the blackbirds
on the other side of
the mesh
go unacknowledged

that searing singularity

it feels like the time
before i ever loved

that searing singularity
that weighty waiting

the only difference
being i don't have
that crazy desire
to love another

it's like i've been
reborn w/ out a heart

just lustful blood
& dusty days
of nothing much

the master of waiting

as you write out a $95 check to renew yr
registration
as you stir the can of baked beans in the pot
as you masturbate to a girl from high school you
dated
as you punch out another few poems
as you make another appointment w/ the
doctor's office
as you boil water for tea
as you take vitamins & high blood pressure
medication
as you make out a grocery list
as you gather dirty laundry
as you fill the cat's water bowl,
etc…

the same spider still sits upon the wall
w/ no movement whatsoever
an eight-legged sage
the embodiment of patience

the still bitter tongue

in my boyhood
the vapors of
the neighbor's dinner
wafting thru
the mesh
of the screen
into the summer air
always smelled better
than our own food

perhaps it was the lack
of conversation
& banishment of laughter
at our own table

& the way
those kitchen walls
seemed to close in
& descent of
the ceiling

that transformed our meals
into something foul
like the odor of old meat
sitting in the trash compactor

to chase ghosts

i'd rather present
you w/ a bouquet of bile
than one of flowers

to braille yr inner scars is my
form of foreplay

to chase ghosts together
thru the night

to taste a spear of dead grass
that grew at yr childhood
home

would far surpass that
petty ugly thing
called touch

the profile of childhood

while driving down
this unfamiliar road
i saw this little boy
& this little girl
playing on the sidewalk
this boy was standing
over this girl
while she was lying
on her back on the
sidewalk in front
of an old house
this boy had a piece
of thick chalk
in his tiny hand
& he was tracing
this girl's shape
they were both
smiling as they
played this game
i could only assume
later that evening
they would get called
into their houses
& get tucked into bed
never realizing
what their game had
triggered in my head
as i passed unnoticed
37 years old this year
& my childhood feels
almost as real as that
flat chalk outline
on the gray cement

some of the dust
occasionally lifted
by the passing winds

until Loss moaned his name

night by night, part by part
the woman he was w/
eventually transformed

her pair of tiny wrists
becoming rivers of Desertion

her arching spine
a bow of Abandonment

the roots of her hair
the threads of Retreat

each rib of the cage
a baton of Betrayal...

until the complete shape
of Absence shuddered
beneath him & Loss
moaned his name

a few years in

we were at the bar
as usual
sharing a smoke
when we noticed
a friend crying
we asked her what's wrong
she told us she was lonely
that she wanted to be in love
that she wanted intimacy like ours
& we both consoled her
but what i really wanted
to do was scream:
i am lonely too
that these cigarettes
are just a brief truce
that this bar
is merely theater for us
that we were wearing
the masks of love
but upon returning
to the dark wings
off-stage at home
our pale unmasked
faces of hate
would glow in the dark
& our dialogue be full of
nothing but venom

a myth

maybe
yr demons
don't exist

maybe they're
yr hideous angels
clawing at you
in the dark

b/c you've
starved them

a thousand cab rides away

do you ever feel like not going home?
like you'd die if you went home?
if you faced the four silent walls of each room?
do you ever feel like you'd do anything
not to be home some nights?
whatever the cost?
you'd go broke just to stay away?
did you ever feel like screaming
or crying b/c the steps
towards home are full of pain?
unbearable pain?
yr life full of pain?
did you ever want to just follow
a stranger in the crowd?
go wherever they go as long as it's anywhere
away from yr path home?
tonight i would've bought 29 meals,
taken 40 cab rides,
sat in the bookstore all night
not even reading
just staring out of the dark window
at the city lights just not to go home
did you ever feel like not going home?
maybe you don't mind going home
maybe you don't get me
maybe you don't get that a cab ride
or 1,000 cab rides makes no difference
i wish i could be like you
i wish i wanted to go home
i wish i was dying to go home

among the pines

when i was five
after a snowstorm
i 'd bundle up
& go outside
in the backyard
& sit in the doghouse
w/ my german shepard
on an old slab of rug
as the wind whipped
& icy flakes ticked
against the old wood
we'd huddle for hours
in our little fort
peacefully among pines
until i was screamed at
to come back inside
inevitably imprisoned
for the night
beneath that big roof

bloody phantom planet

ghosts aren't
invisible
or made of strange
otherworldly
vapors
look around
you
every occupied
house
is
haunted
&
ghosts are
made
of meat
boo,
motherfucker

bugs climb my abyss

there
are
kafkaroaches
running
up
&
down
my
arms
while
i
lay
in
my
sartretude

their
absurd
antennae
itching
my
nothingness

busted & awake

one
night
while
walking
across
the
room

his
eyes
fell
down
inside
his
body

&
he
discovered

buried
in
the
ice

the
screaming
mouths
of
poems

celebration

the anniversary of my pain is every day
it started before birth when i was nothing
even my nothingness was painful
& now that i'm something it's painful
the anniversary of my pain is every day
it started before i ever loved
to not have had yet loved was painful
but when i was in love it was painful
& now that i'm in between love it's painful
the anniversary of my pain is every day
walking across the floor for a glass of water is
painful
stirring pinto beans in a pot is painful
pulling off socks & pulling up socks is painful
the anniversary of my pain is every day
the old four walls are painful
the old blue sky is painful
the anniversary of my pain is every day
writing angry long-hand letters to god is painful
praying on my knees is painful
answered & unanswered prayers are painful
the anniversary of my pain is every day
in my mother's womb it was painful
at my mother's grave it was painful
all the shit in between the two poles is painful
now that i'm something, when i was nothing
all of it's painful
the anniversary of my pain is every day

death & the poetry machine

people always
complain
to me about
writer's block

i don't understand
this phenomenon

a while back
a friend gave me this
old typewriter

one night i decided to
place a skull
on top of it

resting where
the blank page
would be
the empty sockets
stared back at me
the jaw hovering
over the tiers of keys

maybe they wouldn't be
lost for words
if this skinless head
greeted them
before they sat
down to write

but no, they neither
see death nor life

does it fool you, does it rob you?

the face
of the sun
is just
a cheap mask
the
VOID
wears
like
a
thief

robbing us
of
Truth

which
is:

out
there
beyond

is
Nothing

flipping thru frames

you flip thru snapshots
you feel jealous at how intimate
this couple seems
the imprints of her red mouth
forever up & down his cheek
their heads always temple-to-temple
as if inventing their future
the eternal cigarette they always
seem to be sharing
their hands always lifting
a drink to one another
then you summon the un-captured images
dark war-paint beneath their eyes
shards of broken glass in their fists
like makeshift shanks
the chalk outline of their love on the floor

happy fucking new year

as i was
pinning up
a new calendar
i imagined
the maggots
laughing
their goddamn
asses off at
the propaganda
of the
future

if only we can die like this

as the cancer glides around the glass slide
as the unsteady peaks weaken towards a flat line
as the flesh no longer stretches but rather folds
as the bones rise like islands in the weary meat

the leaves release themselves from the tree
after a long summer's reign
surrendering their green
their points still intact not curled like hands
grappling to save themselves
just this calm slow shower of majestic reds
dropping thru beautiful trapdoors in the wind

if only we could die like this —
like old resigned kings on fire
leaping from the world's arms

magnus opus

he
hanged
himself
using
a
stack
of
his
own
books
as
a
platform

what
was
poetry
compared
to
a
silent
blue
tongue?

margin to fucking margin

don't just
bleed
on the
keyboard
pick up
the whole
machine
& drown it
in a tub
of yr blood
then
spread
yr fingers
over that
red
typewriter
making every
page
stained
margin
to
margin
as it rolls
thru

graffiti for mute angels

tonight i think of elliott smith
pressing the large blade thru
the braid of his heart-veins

tonight i think of the mississippi
gathering w/ in the branches
of jeff buckley's lungs

tonight i think of kurt cobain
double-fisting the barrels
of the hypo & rifle

tonight i think of amy winehouse
twisting open the second fifth
like it was amber stitches

tonight i think of all the morgue drawers
full of our mute angels

& i slash the alphabet w/ a box cutter
& graffiti the demons' horns
w/ fucking roses

my soul is a broken down valise

i was born
w/ my angel
split open

like a worn
rubber sole

i was born
w/ my angel
dangling

like a busted
wristwatch band

i was born
w/ my angel
slumped down
by my feet

like a muddy
broken down
valise

& nothing else fills

she'd snap selfies of us
licking each other's face
as we leaned on the lip
of the wooden bar
& shout at friends
that we were
going home to DO IT
as i gave her
a piggyback ride
to the exit
but when we returned home
we'd just pass out
our backs to one another
a good foot & half
in between
& the only thing filled
was the shallow pit
on each
side of the mattress

poem about 9/11 i thought i'd never write

a few days after
september 11, 2001
i walked from
penn station all
the way down to
the barricaded
perimeters
of ground zero
in the train station
there were many soldiers
in full fatigues
w/ M-16s slung around
their shoulders
there were lots of
police officers
standing in groups
of four or five
there were crowds of
people w/ opened
faces giving eye contact
everyone's face was
more open
as i walked out &
down 7th avenue
there were candles
burning on street corners
next to don't walk signs
& public mailboxes
there were shrouded
figures holding up
photos of missing relatives
there were photos
of the missing stapled
everywhere
w/ phone numbers

& other contact info
a lot of humans were
missing & wanted back
the stores were open
but mostly empty
i remember a popular
music store deserted
the guy at the counter
just leaning there
knowing that new music
might not quite heal
right now, might not
do the trick
the outdoor cafés held
slim crowds
the humbler ones inside
eating lighter meals
than usual
as i got closer i could
smell something in the air
or imagined it
if i had to name it
it may have been brevity
there were extra garbage
trucks barreling thru
the streets carrying debris
extra police cars cruising
two cops on almost every corner
i saw a man near the stock exchange
hosing soot off the sidewalk
there was ash in the air
when i got to the perimeter
& could go no farther
there were big rigs hauling
girders & things like desks
that could've been in offices
on the 79th floor

young girls were handing
out chocolate chips cookies
everyone's eyes from penn
station all the way down were
opened a little wider
everyone's face like i said
before was open
their bodies more dimensional
especially compared
to the flat billboards
advertisements that held
no spell over anyone then
everybody was slightly on fire
each person was a third smaller tower
size of their own human shape
breathing, looking, waiting

rattle

i read a bukowski letter where he said that
he had 6 teeth extracted that same day
one of them being a tough motherfucker to pull
poor bukowski at 45, sitting at the rattling
typewriter
w/ 6 empty sockets like bullet holes screaming in
his skull
& tonight i imagine those half-dozen busted teeth
i imagine cupping them in my palms & listening
to the click
of chips of bone as i shake them together
i feel terrible pain & wonderful luck tonight,
bukowski
i feel the beautiful ancient roots in my hands

requiem

slowly a few posts
at a time
the white picket fence
transforms into
black iron gates

slowly a few panes
at a time
tall windowed rooms
of sunlight
transform into
a dark cold space

slowly a few embraces
at a time
the warm circle of two
transforms into
the cold curve
of the sickle

& suddenly
you live
alone
w/ the worms

the cats are gone

they're fixing up
the abandoned house
across the street

they've pulled plywood
from the windows

replaced
the rotten roof

& applied fresh
paint to shingles

even a new front door
swings on its hinges

there are no more
twisted trees
there is no more
high grass

the stray cats are gone
& flocks of birds

cars slow down now
to get a look

at the large human trap
beneath the sun

the cuff of doom

sitting on the ledge
of the doctor's table
fidgeting, the new white
patient's paper cover
crinkling beneath my jeans
the doctor finally comes in
to take my blood pressure
she pumps the black ball
the cuff tightening around
the sweaty hinge of my arm
her face gets serious
is it bad? i ask
after she deflates her cuff of doom
it's elevated, she says
are you nervous? she asks
i feel my heart in my throat, i say
i haven't been here in ten years, i add
okay, i'll go check on someone else
& be back in about ten minutes to
take another reading, she says
think calm thoughts, she says
then she closes the door
to the horrible little pink room
my pulse slows down finally
as i stare at a jar of cotton balls
& allow my mind to drift back
twenty-five years ago,
to my two favorite cousins
petey boy & benny
the way they used to bring us
smaller kids out on the lawn
at dusk in the summertime
how they'd set up a semi circle
of old wooden folding chairs
how we'd sit on our legs waiting

the two of them facing us in the center
fireflies flashing in the air around us
& the steady repetition of crickets
then they'd start retelling their
favorite episodes of
the tv series the twilight zone
they'd team-tell each tale
trading off on details & dialogue
i remember i'd forget everything else:
about school the next day, my dog
my friends, my father & mother
i'd lean on the edge of my chair
waiting for the next scene to unfold
my favorite episode was the one about
the camera that took pictures of the future
my cousins would love to watch
our faces as they retold the mysterious
twist of the last scene
that's why we do it benny, petey boy would say
pointing at my wide-eyed face w/
my knees pulled up to my chin
for expressions like that, he'd laugh
then after that benny would play the guitar
& they'd harmonize beatles' songs
moving from one song into another
in the thick summertime night
even back then my favorite was "yesterday"
then afterward, i always felt sad & quiet
in the shadowy backseat on the long drive home
like i had left something behind
Fade. . .
the door swings open
once again the doctor pumps up
the cuff of doom
& we both wait
i keep looking at her face
her mouth scrunches up to one side

like she's almost disappointed at the drop
you were just anxious, she says
it's a lot better than the first reading, she says
but i'd like to keep an eye on it, she adds
as the cuff shrinks back down, defeated

the death of the poet

one day
the maggots
will feast
upon
this
melancholic
meat

maybe
they'll get
terribly blue
on the
sad crumbs
of me

that's what
you get
for feeding
on this poet

weep,
maggots,
weep

the poetry reading

all the poets
were so glad
to meet
each other

soft palms
cupping
more
soft palms

hands that
never strangled
the abc's

that didn't have
the indelible
black juice
beneath their
cuticles

i walked out
before the
the first reader
hit the podium

those palms
a prediction
of the poems

the truce

i remember a certain day when i was 4 years old
i remember my brother threw a lamp
i remember how it broke on my sister's leg
i remember how she screamed
i remember the holes in her walls
i remember the accusation YR A WHORE!
i remember the retort FUCK YOU!
i remember my mother & brother & sister
all screaming at once
i remember how it drove me off the couch
where i was trying to sleep
i remember shutting my eyes & running w/my
fist out
i remember screaming BE QUIET!
i remember the sound when my hand went thru
the windowpane of the front door
i remember how they all stopped
i remember my mother whispering:
see what you made him do?
i remember a sudden calmness
i remember one of them examining my tiny fist
i remember the others sweeping up the glass
i remember the trio apologizing over & over
i remember being smart enough to keep it a
secret
that i had not meant to shatter the glass
i remember the piece of cardboard
taped over the empty frame
i remember my hand in a bandage
i remember the red seeping thru the gauze
i remember the brief but beautiful truce

this strange lonesome 40th summer

a
door
is
strictly
a
human
thing

a
way
to
close
out
the
world

people
talk
about
the
metaphorical
door
opening
to
bright
new
futures

but
to
me
a
door
is
a

sad
rectangle

a
rejection
of
the
world

tonight
i
drive
the
streets
alone
&
notice
all
the
closed
doors

one
after
the
other
in
this
strange
lonesome
40th
summer
of
mine

i
want

to
park
along
the
curbside

knock
upon
all
of
the
closed
doors

see
the
white
or
yellow
porch
lights
come
on

the
curtains
swing

the
blinds
turn
the
brightness
from
w/in
throw
itself

across
the
dark
ground

across
the
tips
of
my
shoes

but
i
keep
driving

until
i
get
to
my
own
place
&
then
i
do
the
same

close
this
door

this
strictly

human
thing

this
rectangular
rejection
of
the
world

thoughts while strolling among rows of headstones

just b/c we have a birth date
& a dash after our names so far

just b/c our inscriptions,
so to speak, are open-ended

just b/c we're mobile
w/ a fraction of freedom

just b/c we steer our cars
down marconi blvd at 2:44 pm

it doesn't mean some of us
are really alive

& that our future graves
wouldn't be superfluous,
motherfucker

as faulkner's ghost's laughter echoes thru the steam tunnels

Faulkner wrote
his novel
As I Lay Dying
by hand
leaning on
an upside-down
wheelbarrow
in the basement
of a power plant
during his nightshift
his wrist madly
swiveling over the paper
atop the rusty metal
& crazy bill finished it
in 6 goddamn weeks
& i think of others
complaining today
that they don't have
the right desk
enough space
a better computer
a mountain retreat
a fucking stipend
more motherfucking time

another one for li po

sitting
w/ the cat
& a bowl
of rice
it feels
like the sand
is moving
back
upward
in the
hourglass
as an
endlessness
fills this
tiny
room
wall
to
wall

when we were still young

some summer nights
billy & i would duck down low
in his old monte carlo
& w/ the windows lowered
we'd play a halloween sound effects tape
in the parking lot of a crowded bar:
a cauldron bubbling, witches cackling
wolves baying, bats squeaking
chains rattling, mummies moaning, etc…
the volume just loud enough to cause
people walking w/in earshot
to momentarily cock their heads
or stop & scan the shadows
or quicken their pace
& we'd giggle at our silliness
& sip our beers
as a gravedigger's shovel
scraped the earth
beneath the summer stars

drunk & young

once my parents
threw a party
in their backyard
just a simple bbq
but after drinking
for hours they all
had a water fight
drunk & young
in their early 30s
they threw cups
of water at each other
my father ran in a
& got the salad bowl
some really drunk friend
got the garden hose
people were laughing
dousing each other
my brother & i
watched from a distance
we weren't included
we were too little
after a while we went inside
we were hyper & bored
we ran thru all the rooms
while in my parent's bedroom
we found a pack of condoms
on their dresser
we didn't know what they were
so we opened them
& took the weird
greasy balloons
& filled them w/ water
& hung them from

3 closet doors
then we found a pin
& popped them all
we left puddles on the floor
& ragged stretched rubbers
hanging from doorknobs
& went outside to play...
i'm 37 this year
older than they were then
& i imagine my mother & father
finding the condoms & laughing
not even annoyed at the
water on the floor
just throwing a towel down
under each door
& giggling
& then kissing
maybe even risking
unprotected sex
on that cool summer night
drunk & young
& easy at heart

unwillingly speared

see the newborn
screaming
impaled upon the umbilical
you mother, you father
have speared it
lifted it
from its peaceful sleep
not in the womb
but in the sweet abyss
how can you be proud
as it rides out
on slippery blood
into this war?

Rob Plath files down his demons' horns w/
every poem, major or minor & altho those
bastard points grow back he continues to blow
the shavings from between the keys & hammer
the poetry machine. Check out his website
www.robplath.com.

www.ingramcontent.com/pod-product-compliance
Lightning Source LLC
LaVergne TN
LVHW011401080426
835511LV00005B/382